MEASURING AI'S IMPACT ON MARKETING ROI: ANALYZING AND MEASURING THE IMPACT OF AI IMPLEMENTATION IN MARKETING STRATEGIES

BY
HENRY E. PARKINS

COPYRIGHT PAGE

TABLE OF CONTENTS

3

4

INTRODUCTION

In the dynamic landscape of modern marketing, the integration of artificial intelligence (AI) has emerged as a transformative force, reshaping the way businesses engage with their audiences. As AI technologies continue to evolve, marketers find themselves at the forefront of a paradigm shift, harnessing the power of machine learning, natural language processing, and other AI-driven tools to optimize campaigns, personalize customer experiences, and drive measurable results. This shift prompts a crucial inquiry into the impact of AI on marketing Return on Investment (ROI) and Key Performance Indicators (KPIs) a subject of paramount importance explored in this comprehensive guide.

Overview of the increasing role of AI in marketing

A. **Overview of the increasing role of AI in marketing:** The increasing role of AI in marketing is nothing short of revolutionary. From automating repetitive tasks to providing invaluable insights derived from vast datasets, AI has become an indispensable ally for marketers seeking to navigate the complexities of the digital age. Chabot's enhance customer interactions, predictive analytics refines targeting strategies, and recommendation engines tailor content to individual preferences. Understanding the nuanced ways in which AI influences marketing endeavors is not just a matter of staying relevant; it is the key to unlocking unparalleled efficiency, personalization, and effectiveness.

Significance of measuring AI's impact on Marketing ROI

As organizations invest substantial resources in AI-driven marketing strategies, the need to measure the impact on ROI becomes paramount. Traditional marketing metrics may fall short in capturing the multifaceted contributions of AI, necessitating a new framework for evaluation. The ability to quantify the effectiveness of AI implementations in terms of tangible returns not only justifies the investment but also informs iterative improvements. In an era where data-driven decision-making reigns supreme, understanding the significance of measuring AI's impact on Marketing ROI is a strategic imperative.

Purpose and scope of the book

This book seeks to demystify the complex interplay between AI and marketing ROI, offering a comprehensive exploration of methodologies, best practices, and real-world case studies. Its purpose is to equip marketers, business leaders, and decision-makers with the knowledge and tools needed to navigate the AI landscape effectively. By delving into the specific analysis of Key Performance Indicators (KPIs) and ROI metrics, the book provides actionable insights for optimizing AI-driven marketing campaigns. The scope extends beyond theoretical concepts, offering a practical guide for implementation and continuous improvement.

13

MEASURING AI'S IMPACT ON MARKETING ROI: ANALYZING AND MEASURING THE IMPACT OF AI IMPLEMENTATION IN MARKETING STRATEGIES

CHAPTER 1

UNDERSTANDING AI IN MARKETING

Definition and Types of AI in Marketing

Defining AI in Marketing: Artificial Intelligence (AI) in marketing refers to the utilization of advanced technologies that enable machines to simulate human intelligence, allowing them to analyze data, make decisions, and execute tasks autonomously. In the marketing context, AI serves as a powerful tool to enhance efficiency, accuracy, and personalization in various aspects of campaign planning, execution, and analysis.

Types of AI in Marketing

a. Machine Learning (ML): This subset of AI involves algorithms that enable systems to learn from data and improve their performance over time without explicit programming. In marketing, ML is instrumental in predicting customer behavior, optimizing targeting strategies, and automating decision-making processes.

b. Natural Language Processing (NLP): NLP focuses on the interaction between computers and human language. In marketing, NLP is employed for sentiment analysis, chatbots, and content optimization, allowing businesses to better understand and respond to customer communications.

c. Computer Vision: This AI technology enables computers to interpret and make decisions based on visual data. In marketing, computer vision is utilized for image recognition, visual search, and video analysis, enhancing the visual elements of advertising and user experience.

d. Predictive Analytics: By analyzing historical data and identifying patterns, predictive analytics in marketing helps forecast future trends, customer behavior, and campaign performance. This enables marketers to make data-driven decisions and allocate resources more effectively.

Evolution of AI in the Marketing Landscape

Historical Perspective: The integration of AI into marketing practices has evolved significantly over the years. Initially, basic rule-based systems were employed for tasks like email marketing segmentation. However, advancements in computing power, data availability, and algorithmic sophistication have propelled AI into a more central and transformative role within the marketing domain.

Rise of Big Data: The proliferation of big data has been a catalyst for the growth of AI in marketing. The ability to process and derive insights from vast datasets has empowered marketers to make more informed decisions, target specific audience segments, and personalize content on an unprecedented scale.

Shift towards Personalization: As consumer expectations for personalized

experiences increased, AI became pivotal in delivering tailored content and recommendations. The shift towards hyper-personalization has been a driving force behind the adoption of AI in marketing, allowing brands to connect with their audiences on a more individualized level.

Key AI Technologies in Marketing

Machine Learning (ML): a. Recommendation Engines: ML algorithms power recommendation engines that analyze user behavior to suggest products or content tailored to individual preferences. b. Predictive Analytics: ML models forecast future trends, enabling marketers to anticipate customer needs and optimize campaign strategies.

Natural Language Processing (NLP):

a. Chabot's and Virtual Assistants: **NLP enables the development of conversational interfaces that enhance customer interactions and support.**

Computer Vision:

a. Visual Search: **Computer vision allows users to search and discover products through images, revolutionizing the way consumers engage with visual content.**

Predictive Analytics:

a. Customer Segmentation: **Predictive analytics helps in creating precise customer segments based on behavior, demographics, and other variables, improving targeting accuracy.**

CHAPTER 2

IMPORTANCE OF MEASURING AI IMPACT

The Traditional Approach vs. AI-Driven Marketing Strategies:

Traditional Marketing Paradigm:

In the traditional approach to marketing, strategies were often generalized and based on demographic information. Marketers relied on broad segmentation and mass communication channels, leading to a lack of precision and personalization. Decision-making was often subjective, and the

measurement of success relied heavily on surface-level metrics.

AI-Driven Marketing

Strategies: The advent of AI has revolutionized marketing by introducing data-driven, dynamic, and personalized strategies. AI allows for real-time analysis of vast datasets, enabling marketers to tailor messages, optimize targeting, and automate decision-making. The shift from a one-size-fits-all approach to hyper-personalization has redefined success metrics and necessitated a more nuanced approach to measurement.

Identifying the Need for Measurement and Analysis

Dynamic Nature of AI Impact: AI-driven marketing strategies are dynamic and adaptive, responding to real-time data and user behavior. Traditional static metrics may not capture the intricacies of these dynamic campaigns. Measuring AI impact becomes imperative to understand the fluid nature of campaigns and identify areas for improvement.

Resource Allocation and Optimization:
Efficient resource allocation is critical in marketing. Measuring AI impact allows businesses to evaluate the return on investment for AI technologies, guiding decisions on resource allocation, budget adjustments, and technology investments. It provides insights into which AI applications are driving the most value.

Continuous Improvement:
Measurement is the cornerstone of continuous improvement. By analyzing the impact of AI on marketing strategies, marketers can identify successful tactics, refine

targeting strategies, and enhance customer experiences. Ongoing measurement fosters a culture of adaptability and innovation within the marketing team.

Linking AI Implementation to Marketing Goals and Objectives:

Aligning with Business Objectives:

AI implementation in marketing should align with broader business goals. Measurement helps in evaluating whether AI initiatives contribute to achieving overarching objectives such as revenue growth, customer satisfaction, or market share. This alignment ensures that AI investments are strategically sound.

Defining Clear KPIs:

Establishing clear Key Performance Indicators (KPIs) is essential for effective measurement. KPIs should be directly linked to marketing goals and reflect the impact of AI on specific outcomes. Whether it's improving conversion rates, increasing customer engagement, or enhancing brand loyalty, well-defined KPIs provide a roadmap for measurement.

Demonstrating Value to Stakeholders:

Measurement serves as a means to communicate the value of AI implementation to stakeholders. Whether it's showcasing improved

ROI, increased customer satisfaction, or enhanced brand perception, linking AI efforts to tangible outcomes helps build confidence and support for ongoing AI initiatives.

CHAPTER 3

KEY PERFORMANCE INDICATORS (KPIS) IN MARKETING

Defining Relevant KPIs for Marketing Campaigns

Introduction to Key Performance Indicators (KPIs): Key

Performance Indicators are quantifiable metrics that gauge the success of marketing efforts in achieving specific objectives. Defining relevant KPIs is a crucial step in measuring the impact of marketing campaigns, and AI plays a pivotal role in refining and expanding the scope of these metrics.

Traditional vs. AI-Enhanced KPIs:

a. Traditional KPIs: Metrics like click-through rates (CTR), conversion rates, and lead generation have long been staples in marketing measurement.

b. AI-Enhanced KPIs: With AI, KPIs can be more granular and sophisticated. Metrics like predictive customer lifetime value, personalized engagement scores, and algorithmically optimized conversion rates emerge as AI enhances the depth and precision of measurement.

Defining AI-Driven KPIs:

a. Personalization Metrics: KPIs that measure the effectiveness of personalized content and recommendations.

29

b. *Automation Efficiency Metrics:* **Metrics that gauge the efficiency and impact of automated processes powered by AI, such as automated email campaigns or chatbot interactions.**

c. Predictive Metrics: **KPIs that reflect the accuracy and success of predictive analytics in anticipating customer behavior and trends.**

How AI Influences and Enhances KPIs:

Precision in Targeting: AI **algorithms enable marketers to analyze vast datasets and identify nuanced patterns in user behavior. This precision in targeting enhances KPIs by ensuring that marketing messages reach the most relevant audience segments, boosting engagement and conversion rates.**

Personalization and Engagement:

a. AI-driven personalization enhances customer experiences by tailoring content to individual preferences. b. KPIs related to engagement, such as time spent on a website, click-through rates on personalized recommendations, and social media interactions, are positively influenced by AI.

Optimized Conversion Rates:

AI algorithms continuously analyze and adapt to user behavior, optimizing conversion pathways. KPIs related to conversion rates become more dynamic and responsive as AI identifies and leverages patterns that lead to successful conversions.

Case Studies Illustrating Successful KPI Measurement with AI

Amazon: a. **AI-Enhanced Personalization:** Amazon's recommendation engine, powered by AI, contributes significantly to its success. KPIs, such as product discovery rates and cross-selling effectiveness, demonstrate the impact of AI on customer engagement and revenue.

Netflix: a. Predictive Analytics for Content Recommendations: Netflix employs AI to analyze user viewing patterns and provide tailored content recommendations. KPIs related to user retention and content consumption reflect the success of AI-driven personalization in keeping subscribers engaged.

HubSpot: a. **Marketing Automation:** HubSpot's use of AI in marketing automation influences KPIs such as lead nurturing efficiency, conversion rates, and customer satisfaction. The ability to automate personalized interactions contributes to measurable improvements in key metrics.

CHAPTER 4

RETURN ON INVESTMENT (ROI) IN MARKETING

Understanding ROI in the context of marketing:

Defining Marketing ROI: Return on Investment (ROI) in marketing is a financial metric that measures the profitability of marketing campaigns relative to the costs incurred. It provides a quantitative assessment of the effectiveness of marketing efforts in generating revenue and achieving business objectives.

Components of Marketing ROI: a. Revenue Generation: The primary focus of marketing is often on driving revenue. ROI considers the revenue generated from marketing initiatives against the associated costs. b. Costs: This includes all expenses related to marketing campaigns, such as advertising spend, personnel costs, and technology investments.

Challenges in Measuring Marketing ROI: a. Attribution: Assigning value to each touchpoint in a customer's journey can be complex. b. Long-Term Impact: Some marketing efforts, especially those related to brand building, may not yield immediate returns, making long-term ROI assessment challenging.

The Role of AI in Optimizing Marketing ROI:

Data-Driven Decision-Making: AI empowers marketers with data-driven insights, enabling them to make more informed decisions. The ability to analyze vast datasets in real-time allows for dynamic campaign optimization, ensuring resources are allocated to strategies with the highest potential ROI.

Personalization for Increased Conversions: AI-driven personalization enhances user experiences, increasing the likelihood of conversions. By tailoring content and recommendations to individual preferences, AI contributes to improved conversion rates, a critical factor in enhancing marketing ROI.

Predictive Analytics for Strategic Planning: Predictive analytics, a subset of AI, assists marketers in forecasting future trends and identifying opportunities. This proactive approach allows for strategic planning, minimizing the risk of investing in campaigns with limited ROI potential.

Demonstrating the Impact of AI on ROI Through Real-World Examples

Adobe's Use of AI in Advertising:

a. Contextual Targeting: Adobe employs AI algorithms to analyze user behavior and deliver highly contextual advertisements. This has resulted in improved engagement and higher conversion rates, demonstrating a positive impact on ROI.

Coca-Cola's AI-Powered Content Strategy:

a. Personalized Content Recommendations: Coca-Cola uses AI to analyze consumer preferences and tailor content recommendations. This personalized approach has led to increased customer engagement and, consequently, a positive impact on marketing ROI.

Salesforce's Predictive Lead Scoring:

a. Enhanced Lead Prioritization: Salesforce utilizes AI for predictive lead scoring, prioritizing leads based on their likelihood to convert. This has streamlined the sales process, resulting in improved conversion rates and a demonstrable impact on ROI.

CHAPTER 5

METHODOLOGIES FOR MEASURING AI IMPACT

AQuantitative Analysis of AI-Driven Marketing Campaigns

Defining Quantitative Metrics:

Quantitative analysis involves the measurement of numerical data to assess the impact of AI-driven marketing campaigns. Key metrics include conversion rates, click-through rates, revenue generated, and other quantitative indicators directly related to campaign performance.

40

Attribution Modeling:

a. Multi-Touch Attribution: AI facilitates more sophisticated attribution models by considering multiple touchpoints in a customer's journey. This enables a more accurate allocation of credit to various channels, providing insights into the contribution of each to the overall success of the campaign.

AI-Enhanced Predictive Analytics:

a. Forecasting ROI: AI-driven predictive analytics can forecast the potential ROI of marketing campaigns before implementation. This allows marketers to allocate resources strategically and focus on initiatives with the highest predicted impact.

Dynamic Reporting and Dashboards:

a. Real-Time Metrics: AI enables the creation of

dynamic reporting systems that provide real-time insights into campaign performance. This allows marketers to make agile decisions based on current data, enhancing the overall effectiveness of their strategies.

Qualitative Assessment of Customer Experience and Engagement:

Defining Qualitative Metrics:

Qualitative assessment involves evaluating subjective aspects of customer experience and engagement. This includes factors such as sentiment analysis, brand perception, and overall customer satisfaction.

Sentiment Analysis with NLP:

a. Customer Feedback

Analysis: Natural Language Processing (NLP) can be employed to analyze customer feedback, reviews, and social media comments. Sentiment analysis provides insights into how customers perceive and feel about the brand, contributing to a qualitative understanding of AI's impact.

User Experience Testing: a.

Usability Testing: Qualitative methodologies such as usability testing assess the ease with which users interact with AI-enhanced features. This information helps in refining user experiences, ultimately impacting customer engagement.

Brand Perception Surveys: a.

Measuring Brand Image: Qualitative surveys can gauge changes in brand perception after the implementation of AI-driven marketing strategies. Understanding shifts in customer attitudes contributes to a holistic assessment of AI's impact.

.Implementing A/B Testing and Controlled Experiments:

A/B Testing for Iterative Improvement: a. A/B testing involves comparing two versions of a marketing element to determine which performs better. AI facilitates automated A/B testing, allowing for rapid experimentation and optimization of various campaign elements.

Controlled Experiments with AI: a. Implementing controlled experiments allows marketers to isolate the impact of specific AI-driven changes. This method involves maintaining a control group and an experimental group, enabling a clear understanding of the causal relationship between AI implementations and outcomes.

Iterative Learning and Optimization:

a. Continuous A/B testing and controlled experiments create an environment for iterative learning. Marketers can adapt strategies based on real-time insights, optimizing campaigns for ongoing improvement.

CHAPTER 6

CHALLENGES AND SOLUTIONS

Common Challenges in Measuring AI Impact on Marketing ROI

Attribution Complexity: a. Challenge: AI-driven marketing often involves multiple touchpoints, making it challenging to attribute conversions accurately. b. Impact: Incorrect attribution can lead to misinformed decisions and a skewed understanding of the true impact of AI on ROI.

Data Quality and Integration: a. Challenge: Integrating diverse

46

data sources and ensuring data accuracy can be complex. b. Impact: Poor data quality may result in inaccurate insights, hindering the ability to measure the true impact of AI-driven strategies.

Long-Term and Indirect Impact: a. Challenge: AI's impact on marketing may have long-term or indirect effects that are not immediately measurable. b. Impact: Difficulty in quantifying long-term benefits may undervalue the overall impact of AI on ROI.

Strategies to Overcome Measurement Obstacles

Advanced Attribution Models: a. Solution: Implement advanced attribution models that consider the entire customer journey. Machine learning algorithms can help attribute value to each

47

touchpoint accurately. b. Benefits: Improved accuracy in attributing conversions, providing a clearer picture of AI's impact on specific stages of the customer journey.

Data Governance and Quality Assurance: a. Solution: Establish robust data governance practices and invest in data quality assurance measures. b. Benefits: Ensures that the data used for measuring AI impact is reliable, consistent, and representative of actual customer interactions.

Long-Term Impact Measurement Frameworks: a. Solution: Develop frameworks for measuring the long-term impact of AI-driven strategies, considering factors such as brand loyalty, customer lifetime value, and market share. b. Benefits: Enables a more comprehensive understanding of AI's

influence over time, beyond immediate conversion metrics.

Case Studies Showcasing Successful Resolution of Challenges:

Google Analytics 360: a. Challenge: Attribution complexities in multi-channel marketing. b. Solution: Google Analytics 360 employs machine learning to analyze user behavior and attribute conversions accurately across multiple touchpoints. c. Outcome: Improved visibility into the contribution of each channel, leading to more informed marketing decisions.

Amazon's AI-Driven Recommendations:

a. Challenge: Long-term impact measurement of AI-driven personalized recommendations. b. Solution: Amazon developed a framework that includes customer retention metrics, repeat purchase rates, and qualitative assessments of user satisfaction. c. Outcome: A holistic view of AI's long-term impact, revealing increased customer loyalty and higher customer lifetime value.

Salesforce's Data Quality Initiatives: a. Challenge: Data quality issues affecting accurate ROI measurement. b. Solution: Salesforce implemented stringent data governance practices and automated data quality checks. c. Outcome: Enhanced reliability of data used for measuring ROI, leading to more accurate insights into the impact of AI-driven marketing.

CHAPTER 7

FUTURE TRENDS IN AI AND MARKETING

Emerging Technologies and Their Potential Impact

Augmented Reality (AR) and Virtual Reality (VR): a. Potential Impact: AR and VR technologies can enhance customer engagement by providing immersive and interactive experiences. In marketing, this could lead to innovative product demonstrations, virtual try-on experiences, and personalized brand interactions.

Voice Search and Voice Assistants:

a. Potential Impact: The rise of voice-activated devices and virtual assistants presents new opportunities for AI-driven marketing. Optimizing content for voice search and creating voice-enabled interactions can become integral to marketing strategies.

5G Technology: a. Potential Impact: The advent of 5G technology will enable faster and more reliable internet connectivity. This can facilitate real-time data processing, leading to quicker AI-driven personalization and enhanced customer experiences.

Edge Computing: a. Potential Impact: Edge computing brings processing power closer to the source of data, reducing latency. In marketing, this can result in quicker

analysis of customer interactions, enabling more immediate and context-aware responses.

Anticipated Changes in Measuring AI's Impact on Marketing ROI:

Enhanced Attribution Models:

a. Change: Attribution models are likely to become more sophisticated, incorporating advanced machine learning algorithms for precise tracking of customer touchpoints. b. Impact: Improved accuracy in attributing conversions to the right channels, providing a more nuanced understanding of AI's contribution to ROI.

Integrated Analytics Platforms:

a. Change: Integrated analytics platforms will become more prevalent, allowing seamless analysis of data from various sources. b. Impact: Marketers will have a comprehensive view of the customer journey, enabling better measurement and optimization of AI-driven strategies.

Predictive ROI Modeling: a. Change: AI-driven predictive modeling will play a more prominent role in forecasting ROI. b. Impact: Marketers can anticipate the potential impact of AI-driven initiatives before implementation, aiding in strategic decision-making.

Preparing for the Future Recommendations for Marketers

Invest in AI Education and Training:

a. Recommendation: Continuous education and training on emerging AI technologies and marketing trends. b. Rationale: Marketers need to stay informed about the evolving landscape to leverage new tools effectively.

Adopt an Agile and Experimentative Mindset:

a. Recommendation: Embrace agility and a culture of experimentation. b. Rationale: The dynamic nature of AI and marketing requires a willingness to adapt quickly and test innovative strategies.

Prioritize Data Privacy and Ethical AI Practices:

a. Recommendation: Prioritize customer data privacy and adhere to ethical AI practices. b. Rationale: Trust is paramount in AI-driven marketing. Respect for privacy and ethical practices will enhance customer trust and brand reputation.

Collaborate Across Disciplines:

a. Recommendation: Foster collaboration between marketing, data science, and IT teams. b. Rationale: Effective implementation of AI in marketing requires interdisciplinary collaboration to align strategies with technical capabilities.

Stay Customer-Centric:

a. Recommendation: Maintain a customer-centric approach in AI implementations. b. Rationale:

57

Understanding and prioritizing customer needs ensures that AI applications enhance rather than disrupt the customer experience.

CHAPTER 8

PRACTICAL IMPLEMENTATION GUIDE

As we navigate the dynamic landscape of AI-driven marketing, it is crucial to provide a practical implementation guide for marketers. This chapter aims to equip marketing professionals with actionable steps and insights to effectively measure and optimize AI's impact on Key Performance Indicators (KPIs) and Return on Investment (ROI).

Emerging Technologies and Their Potential Impact

Augmented Reality (AR) and Virtual Reality (VR):

a. Implementation Steps:

Explore how AR and VR can enhance customer experiences in your industry.

Experiment with AR/VR content creation to engage users in novel ways.

Voice Search and Voice Assistants:
a. Implementation Steps:

Optimize content for voice search to align with changing search patterns.

Incorporate voice-enabled interactions into customer touchpoints for a seamless experience.

60

5G Technology: a. Implementation Steps:

Monitor the rollout of 5G in your target markets and adapt content for faster delivery.

Leverage the increased connectivity for real-time personalization and data processing.

Edge Computing: a. Implementation Steps:

Investigate how edge computing can enhance the speed of data processing in your marketing stack.

Collaborate with IT teams to integrate edge computing solutions for faster, more responsive campaigns.

Anticipated Changes in Measuring AI's Impact on Marketing ROI:

Enhanced Attribution Models:

a. Implementation Steps:

Explore AI-powered attribution models provided by analytics platforms.

Collaborate with data science teams to customize attribution models based on your specific customer journey.

Integrated Analytics Platforms:

a. Implementation Steps:

Consolidate data sources into integrated analytics platforms for a holistic view.

Train marketing teams to utilize these platforms for streamlined analysis and reporting.

Predictive ROI Modeling: a. Implementation Steps:

Invest in predictive analytics tools that align with your marketing goals.

Collaborate with data scientists to build predictive models tailored to your industry and audience.

Preparing for the Future: Recommendations for Marketers

Invest in AI Education and Training: a. Implementation Steps:

Establish ongoing training programs to keep marketing teams updated on AI trends.

Encourage certifications and workshops for skill development in AI-related tools.

Adopt an Agile and Experimentative Mindset:

a. Implementation Steps:

Foster a culture of experimentation by allocating budget and resources for pilot projects.

Embrace agile methodologies for quicker adaptations to market dynamics.

Prioritize Data Privacy and Ethical AI Practices:

a. Implementation Steps:

Establish clear guidelines for data privacy within marketing strategies.

Work with legal teams to ensure compliance with data protection regulations.

Collaborate Across Disciplines:

a. Implementation Steps:

Facilitate regular cross-functional meetings between marketing, data science, and IT teams.

Encourage open communication channels to share insights and align strategies.

Stay Customer-Centric:

a. Implementation Steps:

Conduct regular customer feedback sessions to understand evolving preferences.

Prioritize AI applications that enhance rather than disrupt the customer experience.

CHAPTER 9

CONCLUSION

As we conclude our exploration into the intricacies of measuring AI's impact on Marketing ROI, it's essential to recap key takeaways, underscore the significance of continuous measurement, and offer final reflections on the future of AI in marketing.

Summarizing Key Takeaways

Shift Towards Data-Driven Decision-Making:

AI empowers marketers to make data-driven decisions by analyzing vast datasets in real-time.

Key takeaway: Embrace the shift towards a more analytical and data-centric approach in marketing strategies.

Diverse Applications of AI in Marketing:

AI technologies such as machine learning, natural language processing, and predictive analytics have diverse applications in optimizing marketing campaigns.

Key takeaway: Explore the versatility of AI applications to enhance various facets of marketing.

Importance of Precise KPIs:

Defining and measuring precise Key Performance Indicators is crucial for evaluating the effectiveness of AI-driven strategies.

Key takeaway: Align KPIs with overarching business goals for a strategic and impactful measurement framework.

ROI as a Comprehensive Metric:

Return on Investment goes beyond immediate revenue and includes long-term impact, brand perception, and customer loyalty.

Key takeaway: Develop a holistic understanding of ROI to capture the multifaceted impact of AI in marketing.

Reinforcing the Importance of Continuous Measurement:

Adaptability in a Dynamic Landscape:

The marketing landscape is dynamic, and continuous measurement allows for adaptability and optimization in real-time.

Key takeaway: Implement an agile approach to measurement,

68

adapting strategies based on ongoing insights and market changes.

Iterative Learning for Improvement:

Continuous measurement fosters a culture of iterative learning, enabling marketers to refine strategies and improve outcomes over time.

Key takeaway: Embrace measurement as a tool for continuous improvement and innovation in marketing practices.

Customer-Centric Measurement:

Continuous measurement should prioritize understanding and responding to evolving customer needs and preferences.

Key takeaway: Keep the customer at the center of measurement efforts to ensure sustained relevance and effectiveness.

Final Thoughts on the Future of AI in Marketing and Its Impact on ROI

Evolution of AI and Marketing Synergy:

The future holds even more possibilities for the synergy between AI and marketing, with emerging technologies and advanced analytics playing a pivotal role.

Final thought: Stay abreast of technological advancements and leverage AI innovations to propel marketing strategies forward.

Strategic Integration for Sustainable Impact:

The strategic integration of AI into marketing is not a one-time effort; it requires ongoing commitment and

70

integration into organizational workflows.

Final thought: Embed AI as a fundamental component of marketing strategies, ensuring sustainable impact and relevance.

Role of Marketers as Innovators:

Marketers play a crucial role as innovators in navigating the evolving landscape of AI-driven marketing, shaping the future of customer interactions.

Final thought: Embrace the role of innovator and catalyst for positive change, leveraging AI to create meaningful and personalized customer experiences.

In conclusion, measuring AI's impact on Marketing ROI is a dynamic and continuous journey. By focusing on strategic alignment, precision in measurement, and a commitment to ongoing learning, marketers can unlock the full potential of AI in driving impactful and measurable outcomes. As we embark on the future, the collaboration between human creativity and artificial intelligence promises to reshape the marketing landscape, offering unprecedented opportunities for growth and success.

OTHER BOOKS BY THE AUTHOR

USINESS ETHICS AND CORPORATE SOCIALRESPONSIBILITY: CREATING A PURPOSE-DRIVEN COMPANY

SIDE HUSTLE HANDBOOK: EARNING EXTRA INCOME FOR FINANCIAL INDEPENDENCE

A GUIDE TO TRACKING CRYPTOCURRENCY WHALES: SCALE-UP YOUR CRYPTOCURRENCY PORTFOLIOS (10,000X)

BUILDING RESILIENCE AND EMOTIONAL

INTELLIGENCE

INVESTOR'S GUIDE: THE POWER OF FUNDAMENTAL

ANALYSIS OF FOREX TRADING

WHAT BILLIONAIRES DOES TO BECOME WEALTHY:

UNDERSTANDING THE GAME

THE RULE OF THE BILLIONAIRES

DISCOVER SELF DEVELOPMENT BOOKS
A PRACTICAL GUIDE TO FINANCIALSUCCESS: STEPS TO WEALTHAI WEALTH: YOU'RE GUIDE TO MAKING MONEY USING ARTIFICIAL INTELLIGENCE (AI) FROM HOM

THE POVERTY RATE IN AMERICA: THE REALITIES, IMPLICATIONS, AND SOLUTION

Note Page

5..........................Date...............

Use this page for all writing during reading or study.

Note Page

5..........................Date.................

Use this page for all writing during reading or study.

Note Page
5..........................Date................

Use this page for all writing during reading or study.

Note Page

5...........................Date.................

Use this page for all writing during reading or study.

Use this page for all writing during reading or study.

Note Page

5.........................Date................

Use this page for all writing during reading or study.

Note Page
5...........................Date................

Use this page for all writing during reading or study.

Note Page

5........................Date................

Use this page for all writing during reading or study.

Use this page for all writing during reading or study.

Note Page

5..........................Date.................

Use this page for all writing during reading or study.

Use this page for all writing during reading or study.

Note Page

5..........................Date................

Use this page for all writing during reading or study.